WEEKLY WR READER
EARLY LEARNING LIBRARY

In the Sky

The Sun

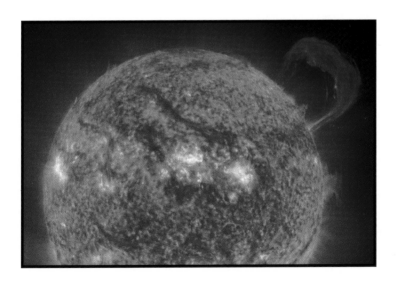

by Carol Ryback

Reading consultant: Susan Nations, M.Ed., author/literacy coach/
consultant in literacy development

Please visit our web site at: www.earlyliteracy.cc
For a free color catalog describing Weekly Reader® Early Learning Library's
list of high-quality books, call 1-877-445-5824 (USA) or 1-800-387-3178 (Canada).
Weekly Reader® Early Learning Library's fax: (414) 336-0164.

Library of Congress Cataloging-in-Publication Data

Ryback, Carol.
    The sun / by Carol Ryback.
        p. cm. — (In the sky)
    Includes bibliographical references and index.
    ISBN 0-8368-6346-1 (lib. bdg.)
    ISBN 0-8368-6351-8 (softcover)
        1. Sun—Juvenile literature. 2. Stars—Juvenile literature. I. Title.
    QB521.5.R93   2006
    523.7—dc22   2005026537

This edition first published in 2006 by
Weekly Reader® Early Learning Library
A Member of the WRC Media Family of Companies
330 West Olive Street, Suite 100
Milwaukee, WI 53212 USA

Copyright © 2004 by Weekly Reader® Early Learning Library

Series editor: Dorothy L. Gibbs
Editor: Barbara Kiely Miller
Art direction, cover and layout design: Tammy West
Photo research: Diane Laska-Swanke

Photo credits: Cover, title, ESA/NASA; pp. 5, 7, 16 NASA; p. 6 © Peter Krohn, www.krohn-photos.com;
pp. 9, 11 SOHO (ESA & NASA); pp. 10, 17, 18 Tammy West/© Weekly Reader Early Learning Library, 2006;
p. 13 NOAA; p. 14 © Gibson Stock Photography; p. 19 NAIC-Arecibo Observatory; p. 20 © Corel; p. 21
© Pegasus/Visuals Unlimited

Printed in the United States of America

1 2 3 4 5 6 7 8 9 10 09 08 07 06

Table of Contents

On the cover and title page: A special camera in outer space took this picture of the Sun.

CHAPTER

Our Shining Star

The Sun is the star closest to Earth. It is always shining on some part of Earth. The Sun never stops shining. When it is night on one side of the world, it is day on the other side.

The Sun is the most important star in the sky. It is the center of our solar system. The word **solar** means "having to do with the Sun." Earth circles, or **orbits**, the Sun. The other planets in the solar system orbit the Sun, too.

The Sun and its family of planets make up our solar system. Earth is the third planet from the Sun.

SUN

NEPTUNE

SATURN

MARS

VENUS

EARTH

JUPITER

URANUS

PLUTO

MERCURY

Even Antarctica, the coldest place on Earth, receives enough sunlight for penguins to live there.

Sunlight falls on all the planets, but Earth has the best spot in the solar system. Earth gets just the right amount of sunlight that animals and plants need to live. The other planets are too close to the Sun or too far away from the Sun for anything to live on them.

Most sunlight goes out into space. Only a tiny part of the Sun's light falls on Earth, but the Sun is a powerful star. Its light can power spacecraft in space. The Sun's light is also bright enough to hurt your eyes. Never look straight at the Sun.

Solar panels on the International Space Station far above Earth collect the Sun's light energy to use for power.

CHAPTER

Fire in the Sky

Like all stars, the Sun is a giant ball of hot gas.
The gas is so hot it explodes and burns, which
makes the Sun shine in space. Every star shines
because of its exploding gases.

We see stars as white spots of light shining in the night sky. **Astronomers** say that starlight comes in different colors. Starlight can also look yellow, red, or blue. The Sun is a yellow star. The Sun looks much bigger than other stars because it so much closer to Earth.

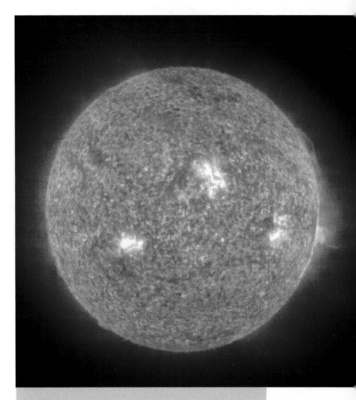

In this picture of our Sun, taken with a special camera, it looks like a burning ball.

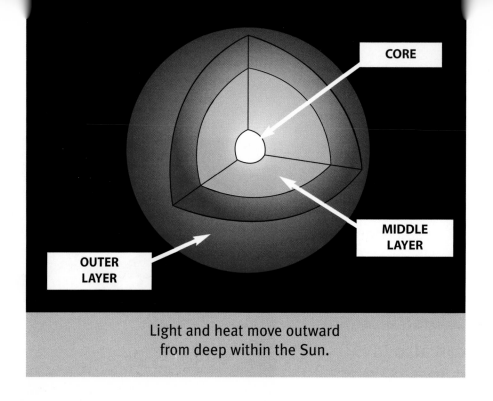

CORE

MIDDLE
LAYER

OUTER
LAYER

Light and heat move outward
from deep within the Sun.

The Sun has three main layers. Gases explode
and burn deep in the center, or **core**, of the Sun.
In the middle layer, light and heat from the
exploding gases move away from the core.
From the outer layer of the Sun, the light and
heat move out into space.

The outside layer of the Sun sometimes looks as if it has freckles. We call these dark spots **sunspots**. Although sunspots look small, they are very large. Scientists say many Earths could fit into one sunspot.

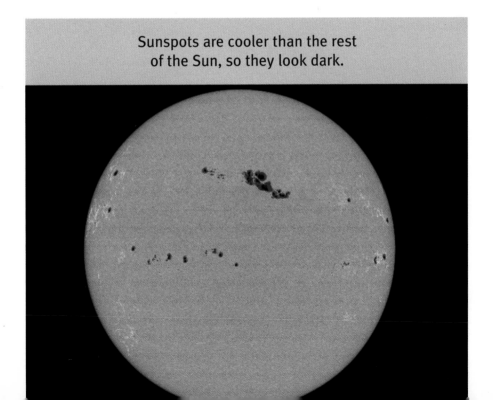

Sunspots are cooler than the rest of the Sun, so they look dark.

CHAPTER 3

A Ball of Energy

Deep inside the Sun, gas is always exploding like many powerful bombs. The strong explosions make light and heat. Light and heat are two kinds of energy that come from the Sun.

The Sun's energy reaches Earth in only eight minutes. Sunlight that falls on Earth helps trees, crops, and other plants grow. Heat from the Sun makes the wind blow and causes our weather. The Sun's light helps us see where we are going. Its heat warms Earth — even in winter.

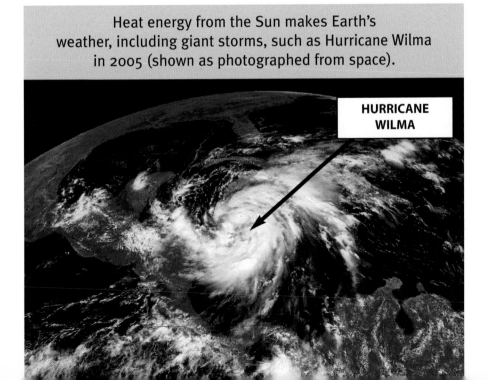

Heat energy from the Sun makes Earth's weather, including giant storms, such as Hurricane Wilma in 2005 (shown as photographed from space).

HURRICANE WILMA

We have gasoline for our cars because of the Sun.

We use the Sun's energy every day, all year long.
We even have oil for our cars and trucks because
of the Sun. Oil formed because sunlight and the
Sun's heat helped forests grow long ago. As time
passed, the forests died and were buried. Oil
comes from dead, buried trees and other plants.
It is a kind of stored energy.

CHAPTER 4

An Amazing Star

Everything on Earth is here because of the Sun. The Sun gives us days and nights and storms and seasons. Can you think of other things the Sun does for Earth?

SUN

EARTH

Earth seems large to us, but it is tiny next to the Sun.

The Sun is much larger than Earth. About one million planets the size of Earth could fit inside the Sun — with room left over! The Sun is larger than all the planets of the solar system put together.

The Sun's large size makes it pull on the planets to keep them in the solar system. This pull is called **gravity**. The Sun's gravity is strong because the Sun is huge. Earth also has gravity, but the Sun's gravity is, by far, the strongest in the solar system.

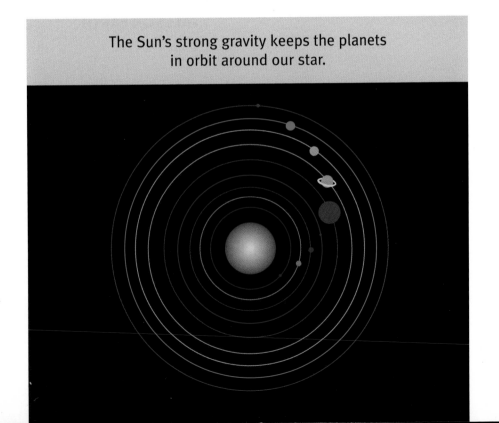

The Sun's strong gravity keeps the planets in orbit around our star.

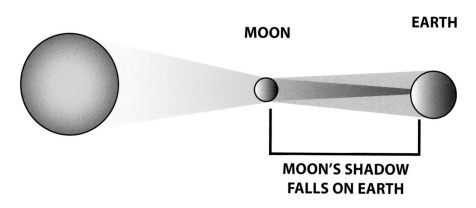

SUN

MOON

EARTH

MOON'S SHADOW
FALLS ON EARTH

You will have to wait until 2017 to see a solar eclipse from North America.

Sometimes, the Moon passes between Earth and the Sun. The Moon makes a sudden shadow over Earth during the day. Darkness falls. Flowers close up. Birds and other animals think it is nighttime. This event is called a **solar eclipse**. Most solar eclipses last about three minutes.

The Sun is an amazing star. It even makes noise! You cannot hear the noise, but astronomers can. They use special tools to listen to the Sun's noises. The noises sound like blowing sand hitting a bell. Noise from the Sun is another kind of solar energy.

The Arecibo radio dish in Puerto Rico listens for noise from space.

How hot is the Sun? Pretend you could build a road made of ice between Earth and the Sun. The road would be almost 2 miles (3 kilometers) wide and 93 million miles (150 million km) long. The Sun is so hot it would melt all of the ice in one second!

Sunlight melts icicles even when the air is freezing.

How old is the Sun? Astronomers think the Sun has been shining for about five billion years. They say it will shine for at least another five billion years. Keep your sunglasses handy!

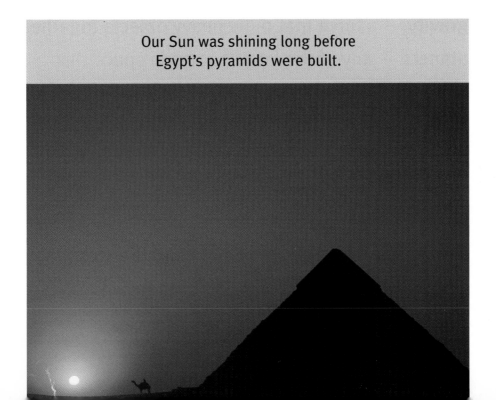

Our Sun was shining long before Egypt's pyramids were built.

Glossary

astronomers — scientists who study the stars and other objects in space

eclipse — a temporary shadow in space that blocks sunlight from reaching Earth, one of the planets, or the Moon

energy — power

gravity — a force that pulls heavy objects together

planets — any of the large bodies in space that circle a star

solar — having to do with the Sun

solar eclipse — the shadow of the Moon that falls on Earth for a few minutes during daylight hours. A solar eclipse happens because the Moon passes between the Sun and Earth.

solar system — a set of planets and the star they circle; our Sun, its planets, and all the other objects in space are affected by the Sun's gravity

star — an object in space that shines by its own power

For More Information

Books

Fun with the Sun. Investigate Science (series).
   Melissa Stewart (Compass Point Books)

Sun. Jump into Science (series). Steve Tomecek
   (National Geographic Children's Books)

The Sun. First Facts (series). Ralph Winrich
   (Capstone Press)

The Sun: Our Nearest Star. Let's-Read-and-Find-Out
   Science (series). Franklyn M. Branley (HarperCollins)

Web sites

NASA Space Place: Why Is the Sky Blue?
spaceplace.nasa.gov/en/kids/misrsky/misr_sky.shtml
Discover why the sky is blue and learn about light energy
that comes from the Sun.

Sun-Earth Connection: Our Star — Our Sun
www.nasa.gov/audience/forkids/activities/
CS_Our_Star_Our_Sun.html
Watch a slide show about the Sun.

Index

About the Author

Carol Ryback remembers saving her allowance to buy a school binder that featured the planets. She still finds outer space and other "scientific stuff" fascinating. A lifelong Wisconsin resident, Carol's favorite dog stars are golden retrievers Bailey, Merlin, and Harley Taylorson. When not stargazing, Carol likes to scuba dive.